WISDOM TREE

Contents

1. **Good Manners**   3
   Good manners will win you friends

2. **Eat Right, Be Healthy**   8
   Health is wealth

3. **Friendship**   14
   A friend in need is a friend indeed

4. **We are Different**   20
   We are different, but we are alike too

   Understanding Myself   26

5. **Cleanliness**   28
   Cleanliness is next to godliness

6. **Do Your Own Work**   34
   Self-help is the best help

7. **Love for Nature**   38
   Nature is our friend. Love nature

8. **Kindness to Animals**   42
   Be kind to animals

Good Manners

Good manners make good children.
Talking politely and listening to others when they speak are good manners.
Saying 'thank you' when someone helps you and saying 'sorry' when you do something wrong are good manners too.

Let us read the poem on good manners.

Good Manners

We say "Thank You"
We say "Please"
And "Excuse Me"
When we sneeze.
That is the way
We do what is right
We have manners
We are polite.

Right or Wrong?

We should say 'thank you' when we sneeze.

We should say 'please' when we sneeze.

We should say 'excuse me' when we sneeze.

Let Us Understand More

When someone gives us something, we should say 'Thank you.'

When we ask for something from others, we should say 'Please.'

When we do something wrong, we should always say 'Sorry.'

We should speak softly.

We should listen to others attentively.

Let Us Do

1. **Complete the words.**

   a. Never talk | b | | d | about others.

   b. Never pick your | n | | s | e | in front of others.

   c. Knock on the | d | | o | r | before entering a room.

   d. When you call up someone on the phone, first tell them who | y | | u | are.

   e. Don't make | f | | n | of others.

2. **Fill in the blanks:**

   a. We should not _____ with our mouth full of food. (talk/cry)

   b. We should greet people when we _____ them. (draw/meet)

   c. When someone helps us, we should say _____.

   (thank you/sorry)

   d. We should _____ people younger than us. (scold/help)

   e. We should not interrupt when _____ are talking to each other.

   (parrots/elders)

3. What should you do?

   a. You pushed Esther by mistake. You say   i. Excuse me

   b. Your aunt has given you a storybook for your birthday. You say   ii. Sorry

   c. You want people to move out of your way. You say   iii. Please

   d. You need your friend's help. You say   iv. Thank you

Let Us Think

Would you like to be friends with a child with good manners or with an ill-mannered child? Everyone likes a child with good manners. We should all try to be good mannered.

What Will You Do?

1. You want a toy. Your mother says no. Will you:

2. You are at the shop. You finished picking up what you need. You have to pay money. Will you:

3. Your friend forgot to bring his colour pencils to school. Will you:

A VALUE FOR ME
Good manners will win you friends.

Eat Right, Be Healthy

We eat to grow and to be healthy. Healthy foods make us healthy people. However, not all foods are good for us. We should learn about foods which are healthy and which are not.
We should eat fruits and vegetables to stay healthy.

Let Us Understand More

Simi is ready for school. She is sitting at the dining table for breakfast. She loves to eat a healthy breakfast—a glass of milk, a bowl of fruit and anything else that her parents make for her.

Simi never skips school because she never falls ill. She is always cheerful and finishes her work fast because she has lots of energy.

She eats healthy food and so she never falls ill and is always full of energy.
Let us learn what healthy food is.

I am milk. I am called a complete food because I give you all the important nutrients. Nutrients are what your body need to grow and become strong.
I make your teeth and bones strong.

I keep you cool in summers.

I make your eyes strong.

We are fruits and vegetables. We give you vitamins and minerals to make you healthy.
You should eat all kinds of fruits and vegetables. Each one of us makes one or the other part of your body strong.

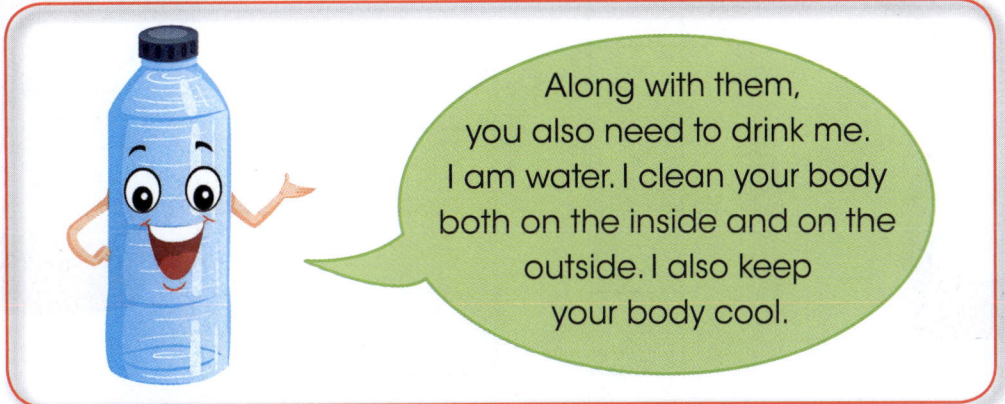

We should all eat healthy food.

Food like potato chips, chocolates and ice creams are called junk food. They are tasty, but not healthy.

The next time you sit down to eat, make sure you check whether your food is healthy or not.

Also make sure that you eat all your vegetables and fruits, pulses, rice and rotis, along with milk and water.

Complete the crossword puzzle:

1. _____ healthy, be healthy.

2. Rotis and rice give us _____.

3. Pulses and _____ give us strength.

4. _____ is called a complete food.

5. Bananas and oranges are _____.

Let Us Think

Eating healthy food comes with practice. We should make it a habit to eat healthy food.

Along with eating healthy foods, we should also develop healthy habits. Some of them are:
- Washing our hands before eating anything
- Washing vegetables before cooking them
- Washing fruits before eating them
- Brushing our teeth in the morning and at night
- Drinking plenty of clean and fresh water

Tell your parents:
Always wash vegetables before cutting them. If you wash them after cutting them, some nutrients will get washed away.

Let Us Do

1. Paste pictures of your favourite foods. Remember to choose from only the healthy foods.

2. **Who among the following children are eating right? Colour the correct box.**

   a. Farah washes her hands with soap before she eats anything.   Healthy   Unhealthy

   b. Nihal always washes fruits before eating them.   Healthy   Unhealthy

   c. Riya loves chocolates. She eats one every day.   Healthy   Unhealthy

   d. Ginny's mom always keeps the food covered. She does not let flies sit on the food.   Healthy   Unhealthy

   e. Ali cleans his water bottle every day before filling it with water.   Healthy   Unhealthy

   f. Phileas hates vegetables. He never eats them.   Healthy   Unhealthy

3. **Tick the healthy foods and cross out the unhealthy ones.**

Do you find chocolates and sweets tasty? Remember that germs too find them tasty. So you need to rinse your mouth and brush your teeth well after you eat sweets.

What Should They Do?

1. Tia bought grapes at the market. She should immediately.

2. Rohan is hungry. He should opt for

A VALUE FOR ME
Health is wealth.

Friendship

Everyone has friends.
Friends are fun. They help us. They make us happy. They stand by us when we are sad or bored.
Friends are very important.

The Four Friends

Many years ago, in a jungle in India, a deer, a mouse, a crow and a tortoise were friends. They loved playing with each other.

One day, the deer was caught in a hunter's net. "Help!" the deer shouted. His friends heard him and started thinking of how to save him.
At once, the mouse started nibbling away at the nets.
The crow flew high over the jungle looking for the hunter. "Caw! Caw!" it shouted. "I can see the hunter coming towards the deer," it warned its friends.
The mouse needed more time to cut the net.

The tortoise then went onto the path that the hunter was walking on. It pretended to be dead.
The hunter saw the tortoise. "I am very lucky. I found a tortoise to take home."
Just as the hunter was about to pick up the tortoise, the mouse finished cutting the net. The deer was free.
The hunter saw the deer escaping. He ran after the deer but could not catch it. The disappointed hunter came back for the dead tortoise on the path.
The tortoise too was nowhere to be seen. It too had escaped into the jungle.
Thus, the friends could save each other.

Choose the correct answer:

1. A deer, a _____, a tortoise and a mouse were friends.

2. The _____ was caught in a hunter's net.

3. The _____ cut the net with its sharp teeth.

4. The tortoise pretended to be _____ on the path.

5. The _____ flew over the jungle to look for the hunter.

What do we do with friends?

✓ We share things with friends	✗ We do not fight with friends (even if we do, we should forgive each other)
✓ We help our friends	✗ We do not talk bad about our friends
✓ We play with our friends	✗ We should never make fun of our friends
✓ We care for our friends	✗ We should never forget our friends

Let Us Do

Write down some facts about your friend.

My friend's name is _____.

_____ is my friend's birthday.

He/She is _____ years old.

I like to play _____ with him/her.

I like my friend because he/she is _____.

Drawing Time!

Let Us Think

What do you do with your friends? Circle your answers.

I play with my friends.

I talk to my friends.

I fight with my friends.

I help my friends.

I share things with my friends.

I enjoy with my friends.

What Will You Do?

1. Your friend forgot to get her lunch box. Will you

2. You see your friend crying. Will you

3. Your friend won a prize. Will you

A VALUE FOR ME
A friend in need is a friend indeed.

We Are Different

Do all your friends look the same? Do they all speak the same language? Every person is different from the other. Some are tall, others are short. Some speak one language at home, others speak another language at home. And yet, they are all your classmates. They are your friends, even though they are different.

Let us read a story to understand more.

We Are Different but We Are One

Hi, I am Ravi. These are my friends, Aslam, Gurpreet and Susan. We study in Class 1.

Gurpreet    Susan    Aslam

Don't we all look alike in our school uniforms?
Later, when we are at home, we look and behave slightly different.
Aslam calls his mother 'Ammi' and says 'Salaam'. His grandparents stay in Bengal. Aslam speaks in Bangla with them. Aslam's parents invite us to their home on Id, a Muslim festival. They serve us yummy rosogullas and fish. We love going to their home.

Susan invites us home for Christmas. On Jesus Christ's birthday, we help her decorate the Christmas tree. Her father bakes yummy cakes for all of us. Later, Susan and her family go to the Church to pray. Her parents are from Kerala and they speak to Susan in Malayalam.

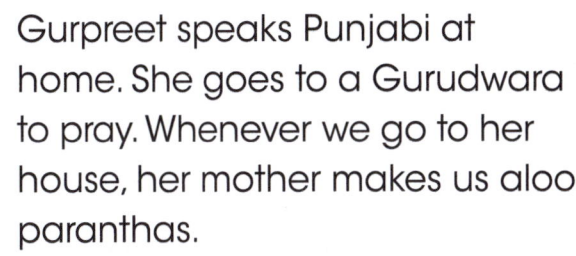

Gurpreet speaks Punjabi at home. She goes to a Gurudwara to pray. Whenever we go to her house, her mother makes us aloo paranthas.

I speak Marathi with my parents. Every year on Diwali, I go to Maharashtra to visit my grandparents. I love eating poha and vada pav there.
We are all different and yet we are good friends.

Fill in the blanks with the correct option.

1. Ravi and his _____ are different.   (Parents/Friends)
2. Aslam speaks _____ at home.   (Hindi/Bangla)
3. Gurpreet prays in a _____.   (Gurudwara/Church)
4. Susan decorates the _____ tree.   (Diwali/Christmas)
5. Ravi celebrates _____ at his home.   (Diwali/Id)

Let Us Think

People in India speak different languages in different places. They speak Hindi in Delhi, Punjabi in Punjab and Kannada in Karnataka. People pray to different gods and follow different religions.
People dress differently and eat different foods. Yet, they are all Indians.

A VALUE FOR ME
We are different, but we are all Indians.

Let Us Do

1. Match the following places of worship to the gods that are worshipped there.

Places of Worship	Gods
a. 	i. 
b. 	ii. 
c. 	iii. 
d. 	iv. 
e. 	v. 

2. Collect pictures of people from different states in their traditional clothes. Paste them here.

3. Just like in India, people from across the world are also different. They speak different languages, they eat different foods and they also greet people differently. Identify how people greet each other in these countries.

England   India   Japan   Saudi Arabia

What Will You Do?

1. Manish went to Chennai. The auto driver speaks a different language. Manish should

2. You have a new classmate. She is from Korea. She looks different. Will you

Fun Time!
On a huge chart paper, each one of your classmates will make a palm print. Later, see how similar all your palm prints are.

A VALUE FOR ME
We are different, but we are alike too.

Understanding Myself

My name is _____.

I am _____ years old.

I stay in _____ (name of the city or town you live in).

I speak _____ (name of the language) with my parents and grandparents.

I have many friends. My best friends are:

1. _____

2. _____

3. _____

4. _____

5. _____

My favourite food is _____. It is a healthy/unhealthy food.

My favourite sport is _____.

I love reading _____.

My parents and teachers tell me that I have to keep my things clean. Here are a few things that I clean by myself:

_____   _____

_____   _____

_____   _____

The last time I went to the zoo, I liked watching _____

_____.

(name some animals)

I promise myself that I will never hurt animals deliberately.

I also promise to take care of nature and not pollute our earth.

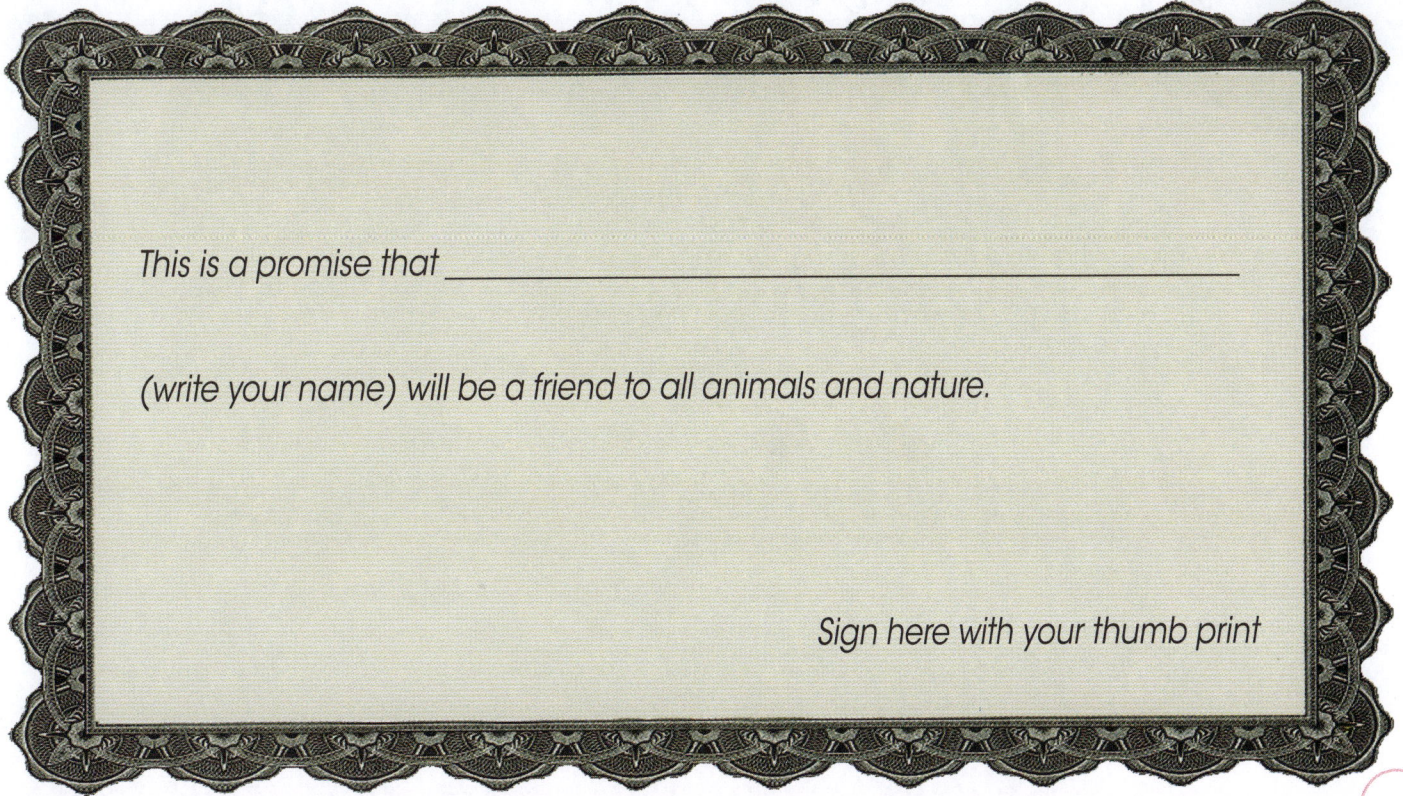

This is a promise that _____

(write your name) will be a friend to all animals and nature.

Sign here with your thumb print

Cleanliness

We all love to have a clean place around us. Dirty places are not nice. We should keep our surroundings clean.

Also, everyone loves a clean person. Would you want to sit next to a dirty person? We should keep ourselves clean always.

Cleanliness keeps us healthy.

John and his family went to see the Taj Mahal. The Taj Mahal is in Agra.

Would you like to be photographed in dirty clothes? John doesn't either. So, he was dressed neatly.

His parents clicked lots of photos of John at the Taj Mahal.

The gardens near the building were also beautiful. The hedges were trimmed and the fountains were clean.

Later, John and his parents went to an ice cream shop outside the Taj Mahal. After having ice cream, they threw the empty ice cream cups into the dustbin.

But the person standing next to them threw his cup carelessly on the road and walked away.

John was shocked to see this.

He called out to the person, "Excuse me uncle, but there is a dustbin near the ice cream shop. You should throw the cup in the dustbin."

The man was ashamed. He picked up the paper cup from the street and put it in the dustbin.

He looked at John and said, "Sorry."

John smiled and went away with his parents.

Answer the following questions. Colour the correct box.

1. John went to clean the Taj Mahal.

2. John went to see the Taj Mahal dressed in dirty clothes.

3. John was dressed neatly.

4. John threw his empty ice cream cup on the road.

5. John politely told the stranger to put the empty cup in the dustbin.

Let Us Think

Cleanliness = Good Health

Cleanliness means keeping ourselves clean. It also means keeping the places around us clean.

When we are clean, we are healthy.

Insects like houseflies and cockroaches grow in dirty places. They poison our food and make us sick. When we keep the places around us clean, these insects will not come near us. We can remain healthy.

Let Us Do

1. Fill in the blanks to complete the good habits chart.

My Good Habits Chart

1. I brush my _____ twice daily.

2. I _____ my hair morning and evening.

3. I clip my _____ every weekend.

4. I always sneeze into a _____.

5. I _____ my hands before and after a meal.

Clues: nails, teeth, comb, handkerchief, wash

2. Tick the images that show clean habits and cross out the ones that don't.

What Should They Do?

1. Hari finished his packet of potato wafers. What should he do?

2. Ali came home with mud smeared all over his shoes. What should he do?

3. Sara goes to school by bus. How should she behave?

A VALUE FOR ME
Cleanliness is next to Godliness.

Do Your Own Work

When we were young, our parents helped us take a bath, brush our teeth, and put on our shoes. As we grow up, we should do some of our work by ourselves. Slowly, we will be able to do all our work by ourselves, just like our parents do now.

Read the story to know more.

Suzan: Mother, please let me help you.

Mother: Why do you want to help me with the work? Go and play with your friends.

Suzan: But mother, I like helping you. That way, your work will get done faster, and you can also play with us.

Mother: How sweet of you my child. In that case, why don't you help me complete the following chores? You are a big girl now, and can surely do them by yourself.

1. Polish your shoes every evening after school
2. Make your own bed once you wake up in the morning
3. Water the plants
4. Fill your school bottle with fresh water
5. Clean your toys

Suzan: Will I be able to do all this by myself?

Mother: Yes, you can surely do all of it by yourself. You are a big girl now.

So, Suzan went and polished her shoes for the next day.

Later that evening, she went to her friend Lily's house. The two friends played with Lily's dolls. After a while, Lily's brother came into the room. The three of them then played 'Snakes and Ladders'.

When it was time to leave, Suzan started putting back the toys in the toy shelf. Lily and her brother ran into the living room and switched on the TV. They sat watching their favourite cartoon show.

Suzan: Lily, aren't you and your brother going to put back the toys?

Lily: Why should we? Our mother will do it for us. Or, maybe our maid will do it.

Suzan: But it was we who played with them. So we should put them back ourselves. My mother says that we should do our work ourselves as long as we can do it.

Lily's mother came into the room and told Lily and her brother that Suzan was doing the right thing. Everyone should do their own work.

Lily and her brother also went into their room to help Suzan put back all the toys.

Suzan: Lily, will you come to my house tomorrow to play?

Lily (smiling): Yes, I will! Also, I will help put back all the toys after we finish playing with them.

Suzan: Bye, Lily.

Lily: Bye, Suzan.

Fill in the blanks.

1. Suzan wants to help her _____. (friend/mother)

2. Suzan's mother suggests that she could _____ the plants. (polish/water)

3. _____ went to _____'s house to play. (Lily/Suzan)

4. Lily did not help to put away the _____. (breakfast/toys)

5. Suzan's mother said, "We should do _____work ourselves as long as we can do it." (others/our)

Let Us Think

We should do our work by ourselves. Only when we cannot do the work by ourselves, we should ask others to do it for us.

Also, there are some kinds of work that are dangerous. Switching on the mixer to make yourself orange juice is a simple task. But you should not do it by yourself because it can be dangerous. You should always ask an adult to do such work for you.

When you do your own work, you become an independent child.

Will you start doing your own work from today?

Let Us Do

1. Make a list of things that you can do by yourself. Write them down here.

    Things That I Can Do By Myself

    a. _____

    b. _____

    c. _____

    d. _____

    e. _____

    f. _____

Now make sure that you do the things every day. Test yourself for a week. Tick the box if you have done all the work by yourself every day.

Monday	Tuesday	Wednesday	Thursday	Friday	Saturday	Sunday

2. Which among the following do you think you should do by yourself? Tick your answers.

    a. Help carry the shopping bags.

    b. Repair the television at home.

    c. Make your bed.

    d. Put away the groceries.

    e. Wash vegetables and fruits.

    f. Fold clothes once they are dry.

What Should They Do?

1. Mahesh broke a glass vase. He should

2. Pooja is at the table for breakfast. She should

3. Rajni has finished painting. She should

Our elders say, God helps those who help themselves.

A VALUE FOR ME
Self-help is the best help.

Love for Nature

The trees, rivers, oceans, deserts, mountains, and the animals and birds that live in them are part of nature.
We should love nature. We should not do anything to harm anything in nature. Cutting down trees, killing or injuring birds and animals, and throwing waste into rivers and oceans are spoiling nature.

Let us read the poem to know more.

Friends

How good to lie a little while

And look up through the tree!

The sky is like a kind big smile

Bent sweetly over me.

The sunshine flickers through the lace

Of leaves above my head,

And kisses me upon the face

Like Mother, before bed.

The wind comes stealing o'er the grass

To whisper pretty things;

And though I cannot see him pass,

I feel his careful wings.

So many gentle friends are near

Whom one can scarcely see,

A child should never feel a fear,

Wherever he may be.

- **Abbie Farwell Brown**

Answer the following questions:

1. What is like a big smile?

    a. The sky ⬚　　　　　　　　　b. The birds ⬚

2. Where is the child lying down?

    a. On the bed ⬚　　　　　　　b. Under the tree ⬚

3. Who whispers to the child?

    a. Mother ⬚　　　　　　　　　b. The wind ⬚

4. Who are the gentle friends near the child?

    a. Wind ⬚　　　　　　　　　　b. Sky ⬚

    c. Sunshine ⬚　　　　　　　　d. All of these ⬚

Let Us Think

In the poem, the child tells us that the wind, the sky, the sun and all other things in nature are his friends.

Just the way we are kind and gentle to our friends, we should also be kind and gentle to nature.

We should not cut trees and plants unless required.

We should water them regularly.

We should not harm animals unnecessarily.

We should not pollute our earth.

We should put all waste only in dustbins.

If we do all of the above, we are kind to nature. This is how we show our love to nature.

Let Us Do

1. Which among the following are activities that show our love for nature?

a. Sid helps the gardener water the trees.

b. Paul uses a lot of plastic covers. He throws them away in the empty space next to his house.

c. Mehrab goes trekking with his older cousins. He loves walking in the hills.

d. Shikha loves to watch the 'Animal Planet' and the 'Discovery Channel' on TV.

e. Gurjeet keeps the windows open to let the cool air into his room. He loves to watch the sun set from his window.

2. Look up at the night sky. Do you see the stars forming patterns? You may see the pattern of a kite, a jug or even a bear. Draw what you see in the space below.

Star Pattern

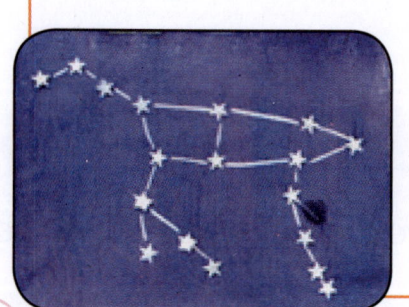

40

3. Go Exploring!

   Visit a garden near your house. Count the number of trees in it. Take a sketch book with you. Draw what you like most about the garden.

What Should They Do?

1. Nikki is walking in a park. She sees a worm. Should she
   a. Scream and run away
   b. Observe the worm from a distance. Go home and check on the internet or an encyclopaedia what kind of insect it is.

2. The weather is lovely. It is not very hot, neither is it very cold. Should Arthur and his friends
   a. play outdoors
   b. play indoors

My Nature Album

Collect things like fallen leaves, twigs and colourful pebbles, and paste them on a sheet of paper. Create your own 'Nature Album'.

A VALUE FOR ME
Nature is our friend. Love nature.

Kindness to Animals

Have you heard that a dog is man's best friend?

Not just the dog, but many animals like the cow, the sheep and the camel help man. We should be kind to all animals. We should not hit them or tease them. We should not harm them.

Nazneen and her brother Feroze came running into the house. "Mother, it is very hot. Can we have some cool drink please?" asked Nazneen.

Mother gave them a snack and cool lemon juice. The children took their snack and juice and returned to the garden. They sat down in the shade of the tree and started eating.

Suddenly, they heard a voice. "Can you give me some water please? It is very hot. I am thirsty."

The children looked around but could not see anyone. They looked up, and on the tree was a little sparrow.

"Can you give me some water please?" requested the sparrow again.

Nazneen and Feroze were surprised. "The bird can talk!" Feroze exclaimed.

Nazneen poured some water in a bowl and gave it to the bird.

"Thank you, dear children. My family and I used to drink water from the lake all the time. But now the lake has dried up. We do not have any place to drink water from," said the sparrow in a sad voice.

The children felt sorry for the bird. Not long ago they too were very thirsty. They understood how the bird was feeling..

The kind children promised to keep water in a bowl for the birds every day in their garden.

Answer the following questions:

1. Nazneen and her brother were _____ because it was very hot.

   (thirsty/tired)

2. The children sat _____ to eat their snack.

   (by a river/under a tree)

3. They then heard _____ speaking to them.

   (a sparrow/their mother)

4. The bird did not have _____ to drink because the lake had dried up.

   (juice/water)

5. Nazneen and her brother were _____ to keep water for the birds in the garden.

   (kind/cruel)

Let Us Think

Animals like the tiger, crocodile and the shark are dangerous. Should we be kind to them too?

Yes. They will harm us only if we go into the jungles or the seas. If we do not go near them, they too will not come near us.

Snakes and scorpions come into people's homes only because people have built cities and towns in places that were earlier their homes. If we do not cut down jungles to build our cities, the animals of the jungles will stay in the jungle and we will all be safe.

Let Us Do

1. **Who among the following children are kind to animals and who are cruel?**

   a. John takes his dog out for a walk every morning and evening. — Kind / Cruel

   b. Rihanna takes her dog out for a walk once in three days. — Kind / Cruel

   c. Mohan climbs trees and shakes the branches till all the birds on the tree fly away. — Kind / Cruel

   d. Binku keeps a bowl of water in his garden for the birds to drink from. — Kind / Cruel

   e. Farooq catches butterflies by their wings because he likes to watch them. — Kind / Cruel

   f. Anu grows flowers in her garden so that she can watch butterflies come near them. — Kind / Cruel

2. **Fill in the blanks to complete the sentences.**

   a. You should be _____ to your pets.

   b. We should keep our pets _____.

   c. We should give them _____ food and water.

d. When the pets are _____, we should take them to a veterinary doctor.

e. We should never _____ our pets.

Clues: tease, clean, sweet, sick, fresh

3. Kindness begins by thinking good about animals. Choose the best word to describe these animals.

Loyal

Beautiful

Cuddly

Wild

Useful

What Should They Do?

1. A farmer's bullock is sick. He should

2. Vani and her friends are walking through a forest. They see a snake. They should

3. Lisa has a pet dog. She should

Art Attack

Create animals with your thumb impressions.

A VALUE FOR ME
Be kind to animals.